01

WELCOME

A WORD FROM DAVID SHEDD

We are engaged in a dynamic global environment, in which the pace, scale, and complexity of change are unprecedented. It is a networked world where what happens in Peshawar affects Peoria—and vice versa..... (a)dapting the Community to this new environment is our fundamental challenge.

- Vision 2015

Dear Colleagues:

No single person or organization can protect our Nation from the many and varied threats we face today. These threats, from looming terrorist plots, to pandemic disease, to the proliferation of weapons of mass destruction, require that we, as a government, work together.

As we have articulated in the Intelligence Community (IC)'s Vision 2015, we must partner with intelligence consumers to meet the need for more timely and unique intelligence. In order to enhance our relationships, it is important for consumers to understand the mission, background, opportunities, and challenges facing the IC. We have published this handbook with this very thought in mind—to broaden your understanding of our work and to help us become stronger partners in protecting our Nation.

Sincerely,

David R. Shedd

David R. Shedd
Deputy Director of National Intelligence for Policy, Plans, and Requirements

HONORING OUR NATION'S VALUES

Civil Liberties and Privacy

Keeping our country safe means more than protecting people and property – it also means remaining true to the principles on which this country was founded. Protecting privacy and civil liberties is part of the fabric of the IC and it helps define who we are. In order to effectively use the tools and information we need to keep our country safe, we must have the trust of the American people and demonstrate that we are worthy of that trust.

The Director of National Intelligence's Civil Liberties and Privacy Office is charged with ensuring that civil liberties and privacy protections are incorporated into policies and procedures at the Office of the Director of National Intelligence and other IC elements. If you have concerns or questions about how the IC respects and protects privacy and civil liberties, we encourage you to contact this office.

Very sincerely,

Civil Liberties and Privacy Office

05

INTELLIGENCE OVERVIEW

DEFINING AND USING
INTELLIGENCE

According to the Intelligence Reform and Terrorism Prevention Act of 2004 (IRTPA), National Intelligence and the term 'intelligence related to national security' refer to all intelligence, regardless of the source from which it is derived and including information gathered within or outside the U.S., that:

- Pertains, as determined consistent with any guidance issued by the President, to more than one U.S. Government agency; and
- That involves:
  - Threats to the U.S., its people, property, or interests;
  - The development, proliferation, or use of weapons of mass destruction; or
  - Any other matter bearing on U.S. national homeland security.

The U.S. Government uses intelligence to improve and understand the consequences of its national security decisions. Intelligence assists policy decisions, military actions, international negotiations, and interactions with working-level contacts in foreign countries. In some circumstances, it can also aid homeland security providers and first responders.

WHAT IS THE
INTELLIGENCE COMMUNITY?

The Intelligence Community (IC) is a group of executive branch agencies and organizations that work separately and together to engage in intelligence activities necessary for the conduct of foreign relations and the protection of the national security of the United States. These activities include:

- Collection of information needed by the President, the National Security Council, the Secretaries of State and Defense, and other Executive Branch officials for the performance of their duties and responsibilities.

- Production and dissemination of intelligence.
- Collection of information concerning, and the conduct of activities to protect against, intelligence activities directed against the U.S., international terrorist and international narcotics activities, and other hostile activities directed against the U.S. by foreign powers, organizations, persons, and their agents.
- Special activities.
- Administrative and support activities within the U.S. and abroad necessary for the performance of authorized activities.
- Such other intelligence activities as the President may direct from time to time.

The IC is led by the Director of National Intelligence (DNI), who is the head of the Office of the Director of National Intelligence (ODNI) and whose duty is to organize and coordinate the other 16 IC components based on intelligence consumers' needs. The other members of the IC are divided into three groups: Program Managers, Departmentals, and Services.

- Program Managers advise and assist the ODNI in identifying requirements, developing budgets, managing finances, and evaluating the IC's performance.
- Departmental members are IC components embedded within government departments (other than the Department of Defense). They focus on serving their parent department's intelligence needs.
- All intelligence personnel in the armed forces are members of the Service IC components, which primarily support their own Service's needs. Each service has at least one major intelligence organization, as well as intelligence officers integrated throughout its structure.

U.S. INTELLIGENCE COMMUNITY

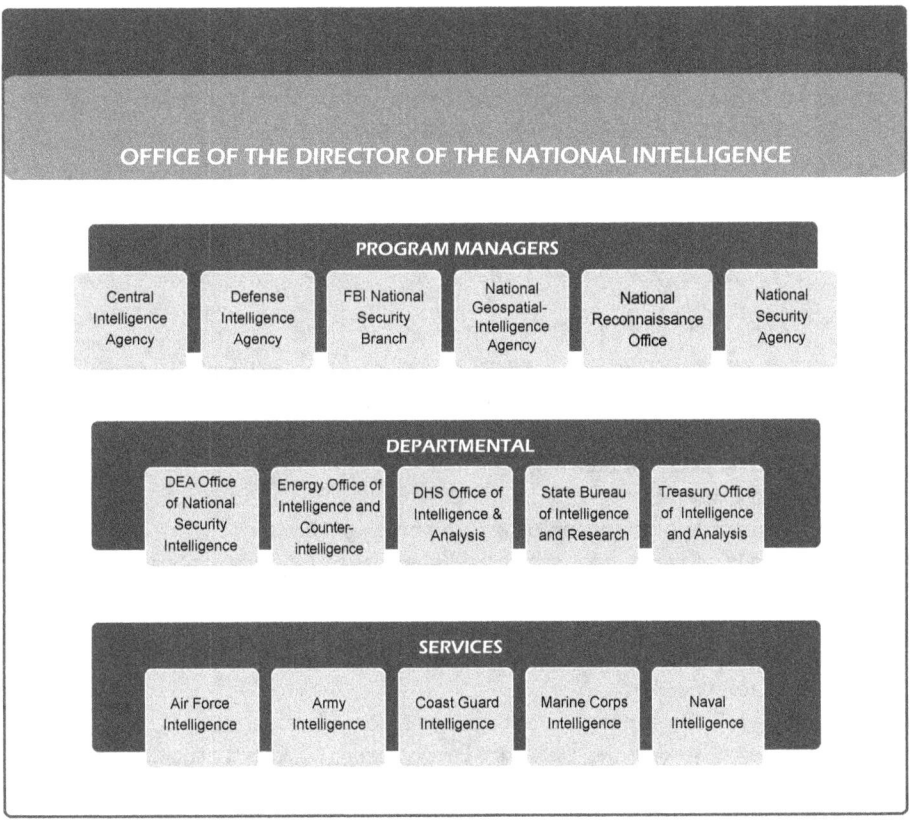

WHAT INTELLIGENCE
CAN (AND CANNOT) DO

Intelligence information can be an extremely powerful tool. It is most useful when the consumer has a clear understanding of what intelligence can and cannot do. While laws, policies, capabilities, and standards are constantly changing, these general guidelines can help consumers make the most of this resource.

WHAT INTELLIGENCE CAN DO

Intelligence information can provide valuable services, such as:

- Providing decision advantage, by improving the decision-making of consumers and partners while hindering that of our enemies.
- Warning of potential threats.
- Insight into key current events.
- Situational awareness.
- Long-term strategic assessments on issues of ongoing interest.
- Assistance in preparation for senior-level meetings that include national security-related subjects.
- Pre-travel security overviews and support.
- Reports on specific topics, either as part of ongoing reporting or upon request for short-term needs.
- Compiling U.S. Government knowledge on persons of interest.
  - The Terrorist Identities Datamart Environment (TIDE) is a classified central U.S. repository of information on known or suspected foreign terrorists.

–	The Terrorist Screening Database (TSDB), which is operated by the Federal Bureau of Investigation's Terrorist Screening Center (TSC), is an unclassified database of all known or suspected terrorist names on which the U.S. Government has information. The TSDB is available to law enforcement officials at all levels of government, and also to Federal Government organizations (such as State Department) that have name screening requirements.

WHAT INTELLIGENCE CANNOT DO

Realistic expectations will help the consumer fill their intelligence needs. Some things that intelligence *cannot* do include:

- **Predict the future.** Intelligence can provide assessments of likely scenarios or developments, but there is no way to predict what will happen with certainty.
- **Violate U.S. law or the U.S. Constitution.** For example:
  - The activities of the IC must be conducted consistent with all applicable laws, to include the National Security Act of 1947, as amended, the Foreign Intelligence Surveillance Act, the Intelligence Reform and Terrorism Prevention Act (IRTPA), the Detainee Treatment Act, and the Military Commission Act.
  - The activities of the IC must also be carried out consistent with all Executive Branch policies, such as Executive Orders, Presidential Directives, and Intelligence Community Directives.
  - All activities of the IC are subject to extensive and rigorous oversight both within the Executive Branch and by the Legislative Branch, as required by the National Security Act of 1947, as amended.

SOURCES OF INTELLIGENCE[1]

OSINT (Open Source Intelligence) is publicly available information appearing in print or electronic forms, including radio, television, newspapers, journals, the Internet, commercial databases, videos, graphics, and drawings.

HUMINT (Human Intelligence) is intelligence derived from information collected and provided by human sources. This intelligence includes overt data collected by personnel in diplomatic and consular posts, as well as otherwise unobtainable information collected via clandestine sources of information, debriefings of foreign nationals and U.S. citizens who travel abroad, official contacts with foreign governments, and direct observation.

SIGINT (Signals Intelligence) is information gathered from data transmissions, including communications intelligence (COMINT), electronic intelligence (ELINT), and foreign instrumentation signals intelligence (FISINT).

GEOINT (Geospatial Intelligence) is information describing, visually depicting, and accurately locating physical features and human activities on the Earth. Examples of GEOINT products include imagery, analyses, maps, and navigation charts. Imagery intelligence (IMINT) is a subset of GEOINT.

MASINT (Measurement and Signature Intelligence) is information produced by quantitative and qualitative analysis of physical attributes of targets and events in order to characterize and identify them.

---

[1] These definitions are intended to be educational in nature and should not be construed as legal definitions.

George A. Custer: GEOINT Pioneer

The idea of using balloons for reconnaissance dated to the Napoleonic Wars, but the U.S. Army did not give it a try until 1862, during MG George B. McClellan's advance on the Confederate capital of Richmond. Though the new "Balloon Corps" enthusiastically promoted this new way of collecting intelligence on the enemy, Army officers, including a young staff officer named George A. Custer, wondered how much the "aeronauts" were really seeing from up in sky. To verify their reports, a reluctant Custer was sent aloft in a balloon. As a result, he became one of the world's first geospatial-intelligence analysts, and viewed first-hand the importance and difficulties of what would later be called the collection-analysis interface.

During his ascent, Custer noted that rebel and Union encampments were hidden from view by trees to block out the blazing sun. Only after intense observation could Custer see camps, fortifications, and an odd artillery piece amongst the trees.

On reporting his findings, Custer received orders to make daily follow-up ascents. Through these daily observations, Custer became expert at locating enemy positions, discerning artillery muzzle flashes, and determining day-to-day enemy troop movement by counting campfires.

Custer's intelligence did not result in a victory for MG George B. McClellan's Army of the Potomac during the Peninsula Campaign. But it did demonstrate the need for subject-matter expertise, and the importance of innovation, imagination, and collaboration between the intelligence collector and analyst.

LEVELS OF INTELLIGENCE

ANALYSIS

The IC publishes three overlapping levels of intelligence analysis: current intelligence, trend analysis, and long-term assessment. In almost all cases, the reports reflect a merging of different sources of intelligence, experience, and knowledge. Analysts choose what level of report to produce and publish based on the data they have available, the urgency of consumers' need for that information, and the degree of vetting and analysis that goes into the report. Each IC component names and distributes its reports differently.

CURRENT INTELLIGENCE

Current intelligence, also known as first-phase reporting, is quick-turn-around, often time-sensitive intelligence reporting or analysis about recent events or newly acquired information. It addresses an issue of immediate or on-going concern. This reporting primarily contains the information gathered from an intelligence source and a brief analysis of the implications or significance of that information, and may include warnings about imminent threats. Current intelligence usually only addresses a single event or issue, and is written to quickly distribute information to consumers.

Example: Country X launched a missile last night. A brief background lets readers know that this was Country X's third launch this year.

TREND ANALYSIS

Trend analysis, also referred to as second phase reporting, contains information on an event or series of events. The report includes an assessment of whether the intelligence is reliable, information about similar events, and background to familiarize the reader with the issue. Typically, this information has been compared with other sources of intelligence and vetted with other experts within the IC. These reports are much more thorough than a first-phase report, and may take weeks or more to produce.

Example: Country X launched eight missiles this year. The report provides a paragraph about the history of Country X's missile program and assesses how the missile program has changed since last year. Missile experts from around the IC have reviewed and contributed to the report.

LONG-TERM ASSESSMENT

Long-term assessment is also known as third-phase reporting. It addresses developments in a broad context, assesses future trends or developments, or provides comprehensive, detailed analysis of an on-going issue, system, or topic. These reports, which can take months to produce, may be coordinated with experts throughout the IC and make projections about the future.

Example: A review of the changes in Country X's missile program over the last 10 years. The report takes into account factors such as infusions of foreign technology and Country X's motivation for producing missiles. In addition, it includes a projection of how Country X's missile program might evolve in the next five years and possible factors which could affect that evolution.

THE INTELLIGENCE CYCLE

The Intelligence Cycle is the process of developing raw information into finished intelligence for consumers to use in decisionmaking and action. The cycle has five steps, each of which drives the next step in the process.

STEP 1: PLANNING AND DIRECTION

Decisions are made regarding what types of information to collect and how to collect it. The National Intelligence Priorities Framework (NIPF) is the IC's process for articulating what issues are important, which then determines how to prioritize the use of intelligence resources.

Consumers can participate in this step by ensuring that their information needs are included in the NIPF process so that the IC understands and incorporates those needs.

STEP 2: COLLECTION

The Intelligence Community gathers the raw data used to produce finished intelligence products. Collection can be from open sources, such as newspapers, or from clandestine sources, such as other people or technical means.

Consumers have a wealth of scientific and substantive expertise and information that they can share with the IC. However, the IC does not task consumer organizations with collection.

STEP 3: PROCESSING

The Intelligence Community converts the information that is collected into a usable format, such as by language translation or decryption.

What consumers can add: Policy organizations have robust processing capabilities that can augment the IC's efforts.

STEP 4: ANALYSIS AND PRODUCTION

Intelligence officers analyze processed information to turn it into finished intelligence. This may include drafting reports, evaluating the reliability of different sources of information, resolving data conflicts, and other analytic services. Intelligence reports typically integrate multiple sources of intelligence and the experience and knowledge of many different members of the IC.

Policy organizations typically have analytic capabilities for their own internal needs, as well as subject matter experts who have specialized knowledge not typically found in the IC. These experts' knowledge and experience can enhance the IC's capabilities.

STEP 5: DISSEMINATION

Intelligence reports are distributed to consumers.

Consumers have two major roles in this step. First, consumers need to ensure that their internal components that could benefit from intelligence receive what they need, within policy, legal, and security restrictions. This responsibility may include facilitating clearances for employees who need the information. Second, consumers need to evaluate the intelligence from their own perspective and provide feedback to producers on whether the intelligence was useful and accurate. The consumer's feedback feeds into the Planning and Direction process, and the Intelligence Cycle continues.

PRIORITIZING INTELLIGENCE ISSUES: THE NATIONAL INTELLIGENCE PRIORITIES FRAMEWORK (NIPF)

The NIPF is the Director of National Intelligence's guidance to the IC on the national intelligence priorities approved by the President.

The NIPF is the DNI's sole mechanism for establishing national intelligence priorities. The NIPF consists of:

- Intelligence topics reviewed by the National Security Council Principals Committee and approved by the President.
- A process for assigning priorities to countries and non-state actors relevant to the approved intelligence topics.
- A matrix showing these priorities. The NIPF matrix reflects consumers' priorities for intelligence support and ensures that long-term intelligence issues are addressed.

The NIPF is updated semi-annually in coordination with IC elements, the National Intelligence Council, and other internal components of the ODNI. Ad hoc adjustments may also be made to reflect changes in world events and policy priorities.

The Office of the Director of National Intelligence and IC elements use the NIPF to guide allocation of collection and analytic resources. In addition, IC elements associate intelligence collection requirements and analytic production with NIPF priorities and report to the DNI on their coverage of NIPF priorities.

21

U.S. Intelligence Organization Profiles

OFFICE OF THE DIRECTOR OF NATIONAL INTELLIGENCE

The DNI serves as the head of the Intelligence Community and is the principal advisor to the President, the National Security Council (NSC), and the Homeland Security Council (HSC) for intelligence matters related to national security. The Director oversees and directs the implementation of the National Intelligence Program. The President appoints the DNI with the advice and consent of the Senate. The DNI is assisted by a Principal Deputy Director of National Intelligence (PDDNI), who is also appointed by the President with the advice and consent of the Senate.

STATUTORY COMPONENTS

The **Office of the Director of National Intelligence** (ODNI) includes several components:

- Four Deputy Directors of National Intelligence (DDNIs), each with a unique focus.
- Centers, including the National Counterterrorism Center (NCTC), the Office of the National Counterintelligence Executive (ONCIX), and the National

Counterproliferation Center (NCPC), each responsible for IC-wide coordination and support.
- Mission Managers for specified countries, regions, topics, and functional issues.
- Associate Directors of National Intelligence (ADNIs), including Chief Financial Officer, Chief Information Officer, and Chief Human Capital Officer.
- A Civil Liberties and Privacy Office, as established by the Intelligence Reform and Terrorism Protection Act of 2004 (IRTPA).

In addition, the Under Secretary of Defense for Intelligence is dual-hatted as the Director of Defense Intelligence (DDI) within the ODNI, and serves in this capacity as the principal advisor to the DNI on defense intelligence matters.

"Today, we face some of the greatest threats that any generation will ever know, and we must not be slow in confronting them. We must continue to emphasize integration across the Community to better serve our customers, provide frank, unencumbered analysis, and strengthen collection capabilities that continue to penetrate the seemingly impenetrable."
– DNI McConnell

SELECTED COMPONENTS OF THE ODNI

NATIONAL COUNTERTERRORISM CENTER

The **National Counterterrorism Center** (NCTC), which resides within the ODNI, has primary responsibility within the U.S. Government for counterterrorism intelligence analysis and counterterrorism strategic operational planning.

NCTC's components

- **Directorate of Intelligence** leads the production and integration of counterterrorism analysis for the U.S. Government.
- **Directorate of Strategic Operational Planning** directs the U.S. Government's planning efforts to focus all elements of national power against the terrorist threat.
- **Directorate of Mission Management** provides strategic management of all national intelligence related to the IC's counterterrorism mission to set analytic and collection priorities; advance analytic tradecraft and training; and lead strategic planning, evaluation and budgeting.
- **Directorate of Information Sharing and Knowledge Development** ensures Federal Government agencies can access the information they need through systems such as NCTC Online (NOL) and the Terrorist Identities Datamart Environment (TIDE).
- **Directorate of Operations Support** provides the common intelligence picture for the counterterrorism community with 24 hours a day/7 days a week situational awareness; terrorism threat reporting; management and incident information tracking; and support for worldwide, national, and international special events.

NATIONAL COUNTERPROLIFERATION CENTER

The **National Counterproliferation Center** (NCPC), which resides within the ODNI, is the bridge from the IC to the policy community for activities within the U.S. Government associated with countering the proliferation of weapons of mass destruction (WMD). NCPC conducts strategic counterproliferation planning for the IC to support policy efforts to prevent, halt, or mitigate the proliferation of WMDs, their delivery systems, and related materials and technologies. This includes both states of concern and, in partnership with the National Counterterrorism Center, non-state actors. NCPC achieves this by drawing on the expertise of counterproliferation professionals in the IC, the U.S. Government, industry, and academia. These relationships foster an atmosphere of collaboration and intelligence sharing in order to protect the U.S.'s interests at home and abroad.

OFFICE OF THE NATIONAL COUNTERINTELLIGENCE EXECUTIVE

The **National Counterintelligence Executive** (NCIX), which resides within the ODNI, serves as the head of national counterintelligence for the U.S. Government, per the Counterintelligence Enhancement Act of 2002. He or she is charged with promulgating an annual strategy for all counterintelligence elements of the U.S. Government. The Office of the National Counterintelligence Executive (ONCIX) is charged with integrating the activities of all counterintelligence programs to make them coherent and efficient, coordinating counterintelligence policy and budgets to the same end, and evaluating the performance of the counterintelligence community against the strategy.

NATIONAL INTELLIGENCE COUNCIL

NIC

The **National Intelligence Council** (NIC) is an all-source ODNI analytic component and is the IC's center for mid-term and long-term strategic thinking. Since its formation in 1979, the NIC has served as a unique bridge between the intelligence and policy communities, a source of deep substantive expertise on intelligence matters, and as a facilitator of IC collaboration. Some of the NIC's core functions are to:

- Produce National Intelligence Estimates (NIEs)— the IC's most authoritative written assessments on national security issues, as well as a broad range of other products.
- Reach out to nongovernmental experts in academia and the private sector to broaden the IC's perspective.
- Articulate substantive intelligence priorities and procedures to guide intelligence collection and analysis.

The **National Intelligence University**, headed by a Chancellor, has responsibility for all Intelligence Community education and training, including foreign language training and policy.

The **National Intelligence Coordination Center** (NIC-C) provides a mechanism to strategically manage and direct collection across defense, foreign and domestic realms.

COMMUNITY ELEMENTS UNDER ODNI AUSPICES

Several centers managed by Executive Agents under DNI auspices serve the entire Intelligence Community's needs.

THE UNDEGROUND FACILITIES ANALYSIS CENTER

The **Underground Facilities Analysis Center** (UFAC) uses national intelligence and non-intelligence resources to find, characterize, and assess underground facilities (UGFs) used by adversarial state and non-state actors. UFAC coordinates IC efforts to detect, analyze, collect, and report on UGF programs in support of U.S. policymakers, warfighters, and the defense acquisition community. The UFAC Director reports jointly to the Secretary of Defense and the DNI through DIA. UFAC is composed of elements from DIA, Defense Threat Reduction Agency (DTRA), NGA, and NSA.

 Open Source Center

THE OPEN SOURCE CENTER

The DNI **Open Source Center** (OSC), under the DNI, is the U.S. Government's center for open source intelligence. The Director of the CIA serves as the Executive Agent for the DNI in managing the OSC. It is charged with:

- Collecting, translating, producing, and disseminating open source information that meets the needs of policymakers, the military, state and local law enforcement, operations officers, and analysts throughout the U.S. Government.
- Helping to enable open source capabilities in other parts of the Government and military.
- Hosting open source material on OpenSource.gov for Government-wide use.

About OSC: OSC produces over 2,300 products daily, including translations, transcriptions, analyses, reports, video compilations, and geospatial intelligence, to address short-term needs and longer-term issues. Its products cover issues that range from foreign political, military, economic, science, and technology topics, to counterterrorism, counterproliferation, counternarcotics, and other homeland security topics.

OSC also collects "gray literature," which is material with very limited distribution, such as academic papers, brochures, leaflets, and other publicly distributed materials.

OSC provides training through its Open Source Academy, consultative services, and personnel exchanges.

The National Media Exploitation Center

The **National Media Exploitation Center** (NMEC) ensures the rapid collection, processing, exploitation, dissemination, and sharing of all acquired and seized media across the intelligence, counterintelligence, military, and law enforcement communities. These tasks include the collection, receipt, cataloging, initial processing, and transmission of information; forensic analysis and translation; and reporting, storage, dissemination, and sharing. NMEC is a DNI Center, and DIA is its Executive Agent.

The National Virtual Translation Center

The **National Virtal Translation Center** (NVTC) was established in 2003 to provide timely and accurate translations of foreign intelligence for all elements of the IC. Its mission includes acting as a clearinghouse for facilitating interagency use of translators; partnering with elements of the U.S. Government, academia, and private industry to identify translator resources and engage their services; building a nationwide team of highly qualified, motivated linguists and translators, connected virtually to the program office in Washington, D.C.; and applying state-of-the-art technology to maximize translator efficiency. NVTC is a DNI Center, and the Federal Bureau of Investigation (FBI) is its Executive Agent.

ASSOCIATED ELEMENTS

PROGRAM MANAGER FOR THE INFORMATION SHARING ENVIRONMENT

The **Program Manager for the Information Sharing Environment** (PM-ISE) is a government-wide organization which resides under the DNI. The PM-ISE is charged with planning, implementing, managing, and overseeing the Information Sharing Environment (ISE). The focus of the ISE is to help all levels (federal, state, local, and tribal) of government and, where appropriate, foreign governments and the private sector, to share and exchange terrorism-related information. The Program Manager chairs the Information Sharing Council (ISC), an interagency body that advises the President and the Program Manager in developing ISE policies, procedures, guidelines, roles, and standards.

CENTRAL INTELLIGENCE AGENCY

The **Central Intelligence Agency** (CIA) is the largest producer of all-source national security intelligence for senior U.S. policymakers. The CIA's intelligence analysis on overseas developments feeds into the informed decisions by policymakers and other senior decisionmakers in the national security and defense arenas. The CIA does not make foreign policy.

The Director of the CIA (DCIA) is the **National HUMINT Manager** and serves on behalf of the DNI as the national authority for coordination, de-confliction, and evaluation of clandestine HUMINT operations across the IC, consistent with existing laws, Executive Orders, and interagency agreements.

CIA is headquartered in McLean, Virginia.

ORGANIZATION

The **National Clandestine Service** (NCS) has responsibility for the clandestine collection (primarily human source collection, or HUMINT) of foreign intelligence that is not obtainable through other means. The NCS engages in counterintelligence activities by protecting classified U.S. activities and institutions from penetration by hostile foreign organizations and individuals. NCS also carries out covert action in support of U.S. policy goals when legally and properly directed and authorized by the President.

The **Directorate of Intelligence** (DI) analyzes all-source intelligence and produces reports, briefings, and papers on key foreign intelligence issues. This information comes from a variety of sources and methods, including U.S. personnel overseas, human intelligence reports, satellite photography, open source information, and sophisticated sensors.

The **Directorate of Science and Technology** (DS&T) accesses, collects, and exploits information to facilitate the execution of the CIA's mission by applying innovative scientific, engineering, and technical solutions to the most critical intelligence problems.

The **Directorate of Support** (DS) delivers a full range of support, including acquisitions, communications, facilities services, financial management, information technology, medical services, logistics, and the security of Agency personnel, information, facilities, and technology. DS services are both domestic and international in focus and are offered 24 hours a day/7 days a week.

CIA is the Executive Agent for **In-Q-Tel**, the nonprofit, strategic venture capital firm chartered to connect the technology demands of the CIA and IC partners' intelligence missions with the emerging technology of the entrepreneurial community.

DEFENSE INTELLIGENCE AGENCY

The **Defense Intelligence Agency** (DIA) collects, produces, and manages foreign military intelligence for policymakers and military commanders. It has major activities at the Defense Intelligence Analysis Center (DIAC), Bolling Air Force Base, in Washington, D.C.; the Missile and Space Intelligence Center (MSIC), in Huntsville, Alabama; and the National Center for Medical Intelligence (NCMI, formerly known as Armed Forces Medical Intelligence Center, or AFMIC), in Frederick, Maryland. Approximately 35 percent of DIA's employees are military, and approximately 65 percent are civilians.

The DIA Director is a senior military advisor to the Secretary of Defense and the DNI. In addition, the DIA Director is the program manager for the General Defense Intelligence Program (GDIP) and, since 2006, program coordinator for the DIA and Combatant Command portion of the Military Intelligence Program (MIP). The DIA Director also leads the Defense Intelligence Operations Coordination Center (DIOCC), which is responsible for coordinating and managing worldwide defense intelligence operations to satisfy the priorities of the Department of Defense (DoD) and the Nation.

ORGANIZATION

The **Directorate for Analysis** (DI) assesses foreign militaries. Its focuses include weapons of mass destruction (WMD), missile systems, terrorism, infrastructure systems, and defense-related medical issues.

The **Directorate for Intelligence, Joint Staff** (J2) provides foreign military intelligence to the Joint Chiefs of Staff and senior DoD officials.

The **Directorate for Human Intelligence** (DH) conducts world-wide strategic HUMINT collection operations. DH oversees the Defense Attache System, which conducts representational duties on behalf of DoD and advises U.S. Ambassadors on military matters.

The **Directorate for MASINT and Technical Collection** (DT) is the defense intelligence center for MASINT (measurement and signature intelligence). It collects and analyzes MASINT, and also develops new MASINT capabilities.

The **Directorate for Information Management and Chief Information Officer** (DS) serves as DIA's information technology component. It manages the Department of Defense Intelligence Information System (DoDIIS) and operates the Joint Worldwide Intelligence Communications System (JWICS).

DIA also operates the **National Defense Intelligence College** (NDIC, formerly Joint Military Intelligence College, or JMIC), a fully accredited educational institution that awards Master and Bachelor degrees in strategic intelligence.

DEPARTMENT OF JUSTICE | **FEDERAL BUREAU OF INVESTIGATION**

NATIONAL SECURITY BRANCH

The **Federal Bureau of Investigation** (FBI), as an intelligence and law enforcement agency, is responsible for understanding threats to our national security and penetrating national and transnational networks that have a desire and capability to harm the U.S. The FBI coordinates these efforts with its IC and law enforcement partners. It focuses on terrorist organizations, foreign intelligence services, Weapon of Mass Destruction (WMD) proliferators, and criminal enterprises.

The FBI is headquartered in Washington, D.C. It has 56 field offices and more than 400 satellite offices throughout the U.S. The FBI also has more than 50 international offices, known as Legal Attaches, in embassies worldwide.

ORGANIZATION

The **National Security Branch** (NSB) oversees the FBI's national security programs. It includes four divisions plus the Terrorist Screening Center (TSC).

The **Counterterrorism Division** (CTD) focuses on both domestic and international terrorism. It oversees the Joint Terrorism Task Forces (JTTFs).

The **Counterintelligence Division** (CD) prevents and investigates foreign intelligence activities within the U.S. and espionage activities in the U.S. and overseas.

The **Directorate of Intelligence** (DI) is the FBI's intelligence analysis component. It has embedded employees at FBI Headquarters and in each field office through Field Intelligence Groups (FIGs) and fusion centers.

The **Weapons of Mass Destruction Directorate** (WMDD) prevents individuals and groups from acquiring WMD capabilities and technologies for use against the U.S., and links all operational and scientific/technology components to accomplish this mission.

The **Terrorist Screening Center** (TSC) was created to consolidate the Government's approach to terrorist screening and create a single comprehensive watch list of known or suspected terrorists. The TSC helps ensure that federal, local, state, and tribal terrorist screeners have ready access to information and expertise.

NATIONAL GEOSPATIAL-INTELLIGENCE AGENCY

The **National Geospatial-Intelligence Agency** (NGA, formerly the National Imagery & Mapping Agency, or NIMA) collects and creates information about the Earth for navigation, national security, U.S. military operations, and humanitarian aid efforts. NGA supports U.S. civilian and military leaders and is part of the Department of Defense (DoD).

NGA has facilities in Bethesda, Maryland (its headquarters); St. Louis, Missouri; Reston, Virginia; and Washington, D.C. It also has support teams worldwide. NGA will consolidate its D.C.-area operations in Northern Virginia by September 2011.

ORGANIZATION

The **Analysis and Production Directorate** produces geospatial intelligence (GEOINT) – the digital and hardcopy maps, navigation charts, imagery, and analytic reports that describe, visually depict, and accurately locate physical features and human activities on the Earth.

The **Source Operations and Management Directorate** collects the data used to create GEOINT from many sources, including national satellite systems and commercial and airborne imagery.

The **Office of the NGA Command Center** monitors matters of high current interest and the daily status of imagery collection and GEOINT support to U.S. domestic and overseas operations.

NATIONAL RECONNAISSANCE OFFICE

The **National Reconnaissance Office** (NRO) was established in September 1961 as a classified agency of the DoD. The existence of the NRO and its mission of overhead reconnaissance were declassified in September 1992. The NRO is the "nation's eyes and ears in space." Headquartered in Chantilly, Virginia, the NRO is a joint organization engaged in the research and development, acquisition, launch, and operation of overhead reconnaissance systems necessary to meet the needs of the IC and the DoD. The NRO conducts other activities as directed by the Secretary of Defense and/or the DNI. The Director of National Reconnaissance (DNRO) is selected by the Secretary of Defense with the concurrence of the DNI and also serves as the Assistant to the Secretary of the Air Force (Intelligence Space Technology).

The NRO's workforce includes personnel assigned to the NRO primarily from the Air Force, the CIA, and the Navy. However, the other uniformed services and other elements of the DoD and the IC are also represented. Another important part of the NRO team includes some of our country's leading aerospace corporations and research centers.

ORGANIZATION ROLE

NRO's organizational goals are to:
- Be a foundation for global situational awareness.
- Provide intelligence on timelines that are responsive to user needs.

The NRO collaborates closely with its mission partners NSA, NGA, CIA, U.S. Strategic Forces Command, U.S. Air Force, U.S. Army, and the Department of the Navy, as well as other intelligence and defense organizations.

Information collected using NRO satellites is used for intelligence and analysis for a variety of tasks, such as warning of potential foreign military aggression, monitoring weapons of mass destruction programs, enforcing arms control and environmental treaties, and assessing the impact of natural and manmade disasters.

The NRO's budget is composed of funds from the National Intelligence Program (NIP) and the DoD's Military Intelligence Program (MIP).

NATIONAL SECURITY AGENCY

The National Security Agency (NSA) is the U.S.'s cryptologic organization, with responsibility for protecting U.S. National Security information systems and collecting and disseminating foreign signals intelligence. Areas of expertise include cryptanalysis, cryptography, mathematics, computer science, and foreign language analysis. NSA is part of the Department of Defense, and is staffed by a combination of civilian and military personnel.

NSA has an extensive consumer outreach system, with representatives in many intelligence consumer organizations in the Washington, D.C., area, in other parts of the U.S., and around the world. NSA's headquarters is at Fort Meade, Maryland.

ORGANIZATION

The **Signals Intelligence Directorate** is responsible for understanding consumers' intelligence information needs, and for the collection, analysis and production, and dissemination of SIGINT.

Operating under the authority of the Secretary of Defense, the **Information Assurance Directorate** ensures the availability, integrity, authentication, confidentiality, and non-repudiation of national security and telecommunications and information systems (national security systems).

The **Central Security Service** (CSS) oversees the function of the military cryptologic system, develops policy and guidance on the contributions of military cryptology to the Signals Intelligence / Information Security (SIGINT/INFOSEC) enterprise, and manages the partnership of NSA and the Service Cryptologic Components. NSA as a whole is known as "NSA/CSS."

The **NSA/CSS Threat Operations Center** (NTOC) monitors the operations of the global network to identify network-based threats and protect U.S. and allied networks.

The **National Security Operations Center** (NSOC) is a 24 hours a day/7 days a week operations center that, on behalf of the NSA/CSS, provides total situational awareness across the NSA/CSS enterprise for both foreign Signals Intelligence and Information Assurance, maintains cognizance of national security information needs, and monitors unfolding world events.

The **Research Directorate** conducts research on signals intelligence and on information assurance for the U.S. Government.

DEPARTMENT OF JUSTICE | DRUG ENFORCEMENT ADMINISTRATION | OFFICE OF NATIONAL SECURITY INTELLIGENCE

The **Drug Enforcement Administration** (DEA) is responsible for enforcing the controlled substance laws and regulations of the U.S. It brings to the criminal and civil justice system of the U.S., or any other competent jurisdiction, those organizations and the principal members of those organizations involved in the growing, manufacturing, or distributing of controlled substances appearing in or destined for illicit traffic in the U.S. In addition, DEA recommends and supports non-enforcement programs aimed at reducing the availability of illicit controlled substances on the domestic and international markets.

With analytical support from the Intelligence Program, DEA has disrupted major trafficking organizations or put them entirely out of business.

Since its establishment in 1973, the DEA, in coordination with other federal, state, local, and foreign law enforcement organizations has been responsible for the collection, analysis, and dissemination of drug-related intelligence.

DEA has 21 field divisions in the U.S. and more than 80 offices in over 60 countries worldwide.

ORGANIZATION

DEA's **Office of National Security Intelligence** (ONSI) became a member of the IC in 2006. Located at DEA Headquarters in Arlington, Virginia, ONSI facilitates full and appropriate intelligence coordination and information sharing with other members of the U.S. Intelligence Community and homeland security elements. Its goal is to enhance the U.S.'s efforts to reduce the supply of drugs, protect national security, and combat global terrorism.

DEPARTMENT OF ENERGY | OFFICE OF INTELLIGENCE AND COUNTERINTELLIGENCE

The **Department of Energy** (DOE) is responsible for U.S. energy policy.

The Department of Energy also has a system of **National Laboratories** and **Technical Centers**, which are primarily operated by private corporations and universities. They conduct scientific research in the national interest.

ORGANIZATION

The **Office of Intelligence and Counterintelligence** (IN) is DOE's intelligence office and IC component. It focuses on assessing worldwide nuclear terrorism threats and nuclear counterproliferation, and evaluating foreign technology threats. This office also provides the IC with access to DOE's energy information and technical expertise.

DEPARTMENT OF HOMELAND SECURITY | OFFICE OF INTELLIGENCE & ANALYSIS

The **Department of Homeland Security** (DHS) is responsible for leading the unified national effort to secure the United States by preventing and deterring terrorist attacks and responding to threats and hazards.

ORGANIZATION

The **Office of Intelligence and Analysis** (I&A) is DHS's headquarters intelligence element and is led by the Under Secretary for Intelligence and Analysis, with guidance from the Homeland Security Council and Homeland Security Intelligence Council. As a member of the IC, I&A is responsible for using information and intelligence from multiple sources to identify and assess current and future threats to the United States. I&A provides actionable intelligence to support national and DHS decisionmakers while working closely with state, local, tribal, and private sector partners. I&A focuses on threats related to border security; chemical, biological, radiological, and nuclear (CBRN) issues, to include explosives and infectious diseases; critical infrastructure protection; extremists within the homeland; and travelers entering the homeland.

Although they are not part of the IC, several of DHS's other subcomponents have extensive interactions with the IC, including U.S. Immigration and Customs Enforcement, Customs and Border Protection, Transportation Security Administration, Secret Service, and Citizenship and Immigration Services.

In addition, the Coast Guard, a DHS component, is a member of the IC.

DEPARTMENT OF STATE | BUREAU OF INTELLIGENCE AND RESEARCH

The **Department of State** is the lead agency for U.S. foreign affairs and is responsible for the conduct of diplomacy. Its intelligence support component is the Bureau of Intelligence and Research (INR).

ORGANIZATION

The **Bureau of Intelligence and Research** provides all-source intelligence support to the Secretary of State and other State Department policymakers, including ambassadors, special negotiators, country directors, and desk officers. The INR Assistant Secretary is responsible for intelligence analysis, policy, and coordination of intelligence activities in support of diplomacy.

INR's functions include:

- All-source analysis of key events, issues, and trends in support of the Secretary of State's global responsibilities.

- Intelligence policy, operations, and liaison coordination.
- Open source public opinion surveys, polls, and media trends analysis.
- Managing conferences and workshops drawing on outside expertise and administration of the Title VIII grant program on Eurasian and East European Studies.
- Directing the Humanitarian Information Unit, an interagency-staffed center created to identify, collect, analyze, and disseminate unclassified information critical to U.S. Government decisionmakers and partners in preparation for and in response to complex emergencies worldwide, and to promote best practices for information management.

INR has approximately 300 personnel drawn principally from the Civil Service and the Foreign Service.

DEPARTMENT OF THE TREASURY

OFFICE OF INTELLIGENCE AND ANALYSIS

The **Office of Intelligence and Analysis** (OIA) was established by the Intelligence Authorization Act for fiscal year 2004. The Act specifies that OIA shall be responsible for the receipt, analysis, collation, and dissemination of foreign intelligence and foreign counterintelligence information related to the operation and responsibilities of the **Department of the Treasury**.

OIA's strategic priorities:
- Terrorist Financing: Over the past several years, the terrorist threat has become far more decentralized in nature, and many terrorist groups affiliated with al Qa'ida now pose a serious threat to U.S. national security.

- Insurgency Financing: OIA will continue to improve its understanding of the insurgency financing, primarily through the Baghdad-based Iraq Threat Finance Cell (ITFC) for which Treasury serves as co-lead with the Department of Defense.
- Rogue Regimes/Proliferation Financing: OIA has assumed an increasingly important role in Treasury's effort to combat other national security threats, including rogue regimes involved in WMD proliferation. OIA will continue to build on its efforts in these critical areas.

ARMY

The **Department of the Army's** IC component is called **Army Military Intelligence** (Army MI). It is fully integrated into Army forces. Army MI's goal is to provide all-source intelligence that is relevant, useful, and timely, to Army and other military personnel at all levels.

ORGANIZATION

The **Deputy Chief of Staff, G-2**, is the senior intelligence officer in the U.S. Army and is responsible for Army intelligence activities. This includes policy formulation, planning, programming, budgeting, management, staff, supervision, evaluation, and oversight. As the Army senior official within the IC, his or her staff is also responsible for coordinating all Army intelligence.

The U.S. Army's operational-level intelligence organization is **Intelligence and Security Command** (INSCOM), headquartered at Fort Belvoir, Virginia.

The **National Ground Intelligence Center** (NGIC) provides the Army with military, scientific, and technical intelligence. NGIC falls under INSCOM and is in Charlottesville, Virginia.

NAVY

Naval Intelligence's mission is to support maritime operations worl-wide to defend the U.S. Naval intelligence professionals, who are all mem-bers of the IC, are deployed throughout the Navy and the Department of Defense. The **Director of Naval Intelligence** (OPNAV N2) reports to the Chief of Naval Operations (CNO) and is the Navy's Senior Intelligence Officer.

ORGANIZATION

The Office of Naval Intelligence (ONI), headquartered at the National Maritime Intel-ligence Center (NMIC) in Suitland, MD, is a major IC production center for maritime intelligence. It produces intelligence on seaborne terrorism, weapons and technology proliferation, and narcotics and smuggling operations. ONI also analyzes foreign naval strategies, capabilities, operations, characteristics, and trends to support Navy, Depart-ment of Defense, and national needs.

ONI and the Coast Guard Intelligence Coordination Center (USCG-ICC) both have a maritime mission, and they share an intelligence partnership that started in the early 1970s. They are identified as the core element of the Global Maritime Intelligence Integration (GMII) Plan. That plan is a component of the National Strategy for Maritime Security, which was signed by the President in late 2005. ONI and USCG-ICC man an around-the-clock maritime watch in the NMIC, which tracks over 18,000 vessels worldwide.

AIR FORCE

The **Air Force Intelligence, Surveillance, and Reconnaissance** (AF ISR) is the Air Force's IC component.

ORGANIZATION

The **Headquarters Air Force A2** is the Deputy Chief of Staff of the Air Force for ISR. He or she provides policy, oversight, and guidance to all Air Force intelligence organizations.

The **Air Force ISR Agency** (formerly the Air Intelligence Agency, or AIA) organizes, trains, and equips forces to conduct intelligence, surveillance, and reconnaissance for combatant commanders and the nation. Air Force ISR is also responsible for implementing and overseeing policy and guidance, and expanding AF ISR capabilities to meet current and future challenges. The AF ISR Agency commander serves as the Service Cryptologic Element under NSA, and oversees Air Force Signals Intelligence activities.

The AF ISR Agency commands several subcomponents, including the 70th Intelligence Wing and the National Air and Space Intelligence Center (NASIC, formerly National Air Intelligence Center, or NAIC).

MARINE CORPS

The **U.S. Marine Corps** (USMC) produces tactical and operational intelligence for battlefield support. Its IC component is comprised of all intelligence professionals in the Marine Corps. Most Marine Corps intelligence professionals are integrated into operating forces.

ORGANIZATION

The Marine Corps' Director of Intelligence (DIRINT) is its principal intelligence staff officer, and is the service's functional manager for intelligence, counterintelligence, and cryptologic matters.

Marine Corps Intelligence Activity (MCIA), in Suitland, Maryland, and Quantico, Virginia, is the USMC service production center. In addition, MCIA supports other services as appropriate. It provides the Marine Corps with intelligence for planning, training, operations, and exercises. MCIA can be tasked to provide expeditionary warfare intelligence to support any national, theater, or operational command in the U.S. Armed Forces. MCIA's analysis and production support not only the Marine Corps, but also the national decisionmaker, theater commander, and operational warfighter.

MCIA is a major production organization for expeditionary intelligence and cultural intelligence.

DEPARTMENT OF HOMELAND SECURITY
COAST GUARD

The Coast Guard is one of the five U.S. armed services. A component of the Department of Homeland Security, its unique blend of humanitarian, law enforcement, regulatory, diplomatic, and military capabilities has five roles: maritime security, maritime safety, protection of natural resources, maritime mobility, and national defense.

ORGANIZATION

The CG-2 is Director for Intelligence and Criminal Investigations.

The Coast Guard Intelligence Program includes the **Coast Guard Counter Intelligence Service**, the **Coast Guard Intelligence Coordination Center** (ICC), and the **Coast Guard Cryptologic Group** (which conducts SIGINT operations under NSA authorities). Actionable intelligence for operational commanders is provided by two **Maritime Intelligence Fusion Centers**, 26 Sector Intelligence Officers, and 30 **Field Intelligence Support Teams** (FISTs).

ADDITIONAL ORGANIZATIONS

Many important government organizations have a relationship with the IC.

Joint Terrorism Task Forces (JTTFs) are FBI-led multi-organization task forces composed of local, state, and federal entities. They were established by the FBI to conduct operations to predict and disrupt terrorist plots. JTTFs are in over 100 cities nationwide; in addition, there is at least one in each of the FBI's 56 field offices. The National Joint Terrorism Task Force (NJTTF), in Washington, D.C., coordinates all the JTTFs.

Fusion Centers combine resources, expertise, and information at the state, local, and tribal levels to improve participants' ability to detect and respond to crimes and terrorism. Fusion centers vary from state to state. However, most include state and local law enforcement; public health and safety entities; and federal entities such as FBI, DHS, and the Bureau of Alcohol, Tobacco, Firearms, and Explosives (ATF).

61

OVERSIGHT

EXECUTIVE OVERSIGHT:
HSC AND NSC

The **National Security Council** (NSC) was established by the National Security Act of 1947. It is the President's forum for considering national security and foreign policy matters with his senior national security advisors and cabinet officials. The NSC also serves as the President's principal arm for coordinating these policies among various government organizations. The NSC is chaired by the President. Its regular attendees (both statutory and non-statutory) are the Vice President, the Secretary of State, the Secretary of the Treasury, the Secretary of Defense, and the Assistant to the President for National Security Affairs. The Chairman of the Joint Chiefs of Staff is the statutory military advisor to the Council, and the Director of National Intelligence is the intelligence advisor. The Chief of Staff to the President, Counsel to the President, and Assistant to the President for Economic Policy are invited to attend any NSC meeting. Other senior officials are invited to attend meetings of the NSC when appropriate.

The NSC drafts, coordinates, and approves National Security Presidential Directives (NSPDs), which are an instrument for communicating Presidential decisions about U.S. national security policy.

The **Homeland Security Council** (HSC) was established by Executive Order 13228 on October 8, 2001. Its purpose is to coordinate all homeland security-related activities among executive departments and agencies, and to promote the effective development and implementation of all homeland security policies. The HSC includes the President, Vice President, Secretary of Homeland Security, Secretary of the Treasury, Secretary of Defense, Attorney General, Secretary of Health and Human Services, Secretary of Transportation, Director of National Intelligence, Director of the Federal Bureau of Investigation, and Assistant to the President for Homeland Security and Counterterrorism. In addition, the Chief of Staff to the President, the Chief of Staff to the Vice President, the Assistant to the President for National Security Affairs, the Counsel to the President, the Director of the Office of Management and Budget, and the Chairman of the Joint Chiefs of Staff are invited to attend any HSC meeting. Other senior officials are invited to attend HSC meetings as appropriate.

The HSC drafts, coordinates, and approves Homeland Security Presidential Directives (HSPDs), which are an instrument for communicating Presidential decisions about U.S. homeland security policy.

Five Decades of Independent Advice

Presidents since Eisenhower have valued the seasoned and independent counsel of the President's Intelligence Advisory Board (PIAB).

In January 1956, President Eisenhower established the President's Board of Consultants on Foreign Intelligence Activities (PBCFIA), in response to a blue-ribbon commission recommendation. By the end of 1956 the PBCFIA's confidential advice constituted perhaps the most important internal influence on American intelligence for the remainder of the Eisenhower administration.

The PBCFIA has been disbanded, reformed, and reshaped over time to serve each President's needs. The PBCFIA was renamed the President's Foreign Intelligence Advisory Board (PFIAB) under President Kennedy, and gained its current name, the President's Intelligence Advisory Board (PIAB), under President Bush in 2008.

EXECUTIVE OVERSIGHT:
PIAB

Unique within the government, the **President's Intelligence Advisory Board (PIAB) and Intelligence Oversight Board (IOB)** is tasked with providing the President with an independent source of advice on the effectiveness with which the IC is meeting the nation's intelligence needs and the vigor and insight with which the IC plans for the future. The PIAB provides advice to the President concerning the quality and adequacy of intelligence collection, of analysis and estimates, of counterintelligence, and of other intelligence activities. Independent of the IC and free from any day-to-day management or operational responsibilities, the PIAB is able to render advice which reflects an objective view of the kinds of intelligence that will best serve the country and the organizational structure most likely to achieve this goal. The IOB, a committee of the PIAB, informs the President of intelligence activities that it believes may be unlawful or contrary to Executive Order or presidential directive and that are not being adequately addressed by the Attorney General, the DNI, or the head of a department concerned. It also advises the President on intelligence activities it believes should be reported to him immediately.

The PIAB currently has 16 members selected from among distinguished citizens outside the government who are qualified on the basis of achievement, experience, independence, and integrity. The PIAB was established in 1956 as the President's Board of Consultants on Foreign Intelligence Activities. It gained its current name in 2008 when the President signed Executive Order 13462; prior to that it was known as the President's Foreign Intelligence Advisory Board (PFIAB).

LEGISLATIVE OVERSIGHT

The U.S. Congress has consistently had oversight responsibility over national intelligence activities. From the 1940s on, the Armed Services Committees and Appropriations Committees exercised oversight responsibility, although their activities were typically discrete and hidden from the public eye.

Following allegations of wrongdoing by U.S. intelligence organizations, the Senate established the Senate Select Committee on Intelligence (SSCI) on May 19, 1976. The House of Representatives followed suit on July 14, 1977, by creating the House Permanent Select Committee on Intelligence (HPSCI). These committees, along with the Armed Services and the Foreign Relations and Foreign Affairs Committees, were charged with authorizing the programs of the intelligence organizations and over-seeing their activities.

The 1980 Intelligence Oversight Act set forth the current oversight structure by establishing SSCI and HPSCI as oversight committees for the CIA. Within the Congress these Committees are responsible for producing Intelligence Authorization bills, which proscribe certain activities of the Intelligence Community. The Senate Select Committee on Intelligence also provides advice and consent on the nominations of certain Presidentially appointed intelligence officials.

The Appropriations Committees, given their constitutional role to appropriate funds for all U.S. Government activities, also exercise oversight functions. Specifically, the House and Senate Appropriations Sub-Committees for Defense produce annual appropriations for national and military intelligence activities via the Defense Appropriations Act.

These Authorization and Appropriations bodies are the principal congressional recipients of IC products, briefings, notifications, and reprogramming requests. They routinely hold hearings on budgetary and other oversight matters.

Other Committees interact with the IC as needed.

FINANCIAL MANAGEMENT AND OVERSIGHT

The Intelligence Reform and Terrorism Prevention Act (IRTPA) provides the DNI with significant budget authorities related to the IC's budget development and ensuring the effective execution of that budget.

The **National Intelligence Program** (NIP), formerly known as the National Foreign Intelligence Program (NFIP), provides the resources needed to develop and maintain intelligence capabilities that support national priorities.

The **Military Intelligence Program** (MIP) funds the unique intelligence needs of the Department of Defense and the tactical forces. It is controlled by the Secretary of Defense, and the DNI participates in the development of the MIP. The Joint Military Intelligence Program and the Tactical Intelligence and Related Activities were combined in 2005 to form the MIP.

69

CLASSIFIED COMMUNICATION SYSTEMS

Frequently Used Terms

ARC: Analytic Resources Catalog (ARC) is a centralized IC repository of analyst assignments and expertise, professional histories and experiences, and personal professional data relevant to analysts' expertise. It includes a searchable repository of contact information known as the Analyst Yellow Pages (AYP).

DoDIIS: Department of Defense Intelligence Information System (DoDIIS) is a DIA-led enterprise that manages the intelligence information technology activities of and provides intelligence technology to the Department of Defense, the combatant commands, and other national security entities.

Fabric: The interconnection between IC computer systems at a given level of security. There is a Fabric for the Top Secret, Secret-Collateral, and Unclassified levels.

IC E-mail: Email between organizations over the JWICS network. Also referred to as ICE-mail or JWICS email.

Intelink: The IC's equivalent of the Internet. Intelink usually refers to Intelink on JWICS (Top Secret), but Intelink also exists on the Secret (known as Intelink-S) and Unclassified (known as Intelink-U) levels.

Intellipedia: The IC's answer to Wikipedia, it is a user-edited compilation of IC knowledge. It is frequently a good starting point for definitions and research. Intellipedia exists on all three Fabrics, but the Top Secret Intellipedia is the most robust version. Intellipedia may be shortened to "Iped."

JDISS: Joint Deployable Intelligence Support System (JDISS) is a software suite that can be hooked up to JWICS, SIPRNet, or NIPRNet.

COMPUTERS

UNCLASSIFIED - LEVEL COMPUTER SYSTEMS

AIN: Agency Internet (AIN) is the CIA's unclassified computer network.

HSIN: Homeland Security Information Network (HSIN) is DHS's unclassified network for developing and disseminating threat information and warnings. Also referred to as HSIN-Intelligence.

LEO: Law Enforcement Online (LEO) is a nationwide unclassified communications network that law enforcement professionals can use to communicate with one another. The FBI uses LEO to communicate with other law enforcement professionals; however, the FBI does not have its own unclassified network.

NIPRNet: Non-Secure Internet Protocol Router Network (NIPRNet) is the Department of Defense's unclassified system.

OpenNet: State Department's unclassified network.

SECRET - LEVEL CLASSIFIED COMPUTER SYSTEMS

ClassNet: State Department's Secret-level network.

FBINet: FBI's Secret-level network. FBInet is the FBI's primary operations network. It does not connect directly to SIPRNet, but can connect remotely.

HOCNet: HUMINT Operational Communications Network (HOCNet) provides information technology, communications, and desktop services for DoD HUMINT needs.

HSDN: Homeland Secure Data Network (HSDN) is DHS's Secret-level communication network. It is designed to share information between federal, state, and local government entities.

SIPRNet: Secure Internet Protocol Router Network (SIPRNet) is a Secret-level network maintained by the Defense Information Systems Agency and used heavily by the U.S. military (and some foreign partners). It is the Secret-level counterpart to JWICS in that it is a communications network, not a terminal. Users must develop their own Secret network or use another organization's terminal to access SIPRNet. Intelink-S (the Secret version of Intelink) runs off of SIPRNet.

TOP SECRET-SENSITIVE COMPARTMENTED INFORMATION - LEVEL CLASSIFIED COMPUTER SYSTEMS

CapNet: Capitol Network (CapNet), formerly known as Intelink-P, provides Congressional intelligence consumers with connectivity to Intelink-TS and CIASource.

CWAN: Contractor Wide Area Network (CWAN) is NRO's Top Secret computer network for contractors.

DIA JWICS: DIA's Top Secret computer network. It is also referred to by DIA as JWICS.

INRISS: INR Intelligence Support System (INRISS) is State Department's TS network.

JWICS: Joint Worldwide Intelligence Communications System (JWICS) is the Intelligence Community's TS-SCI global network. JWICS is a communications network that delivers secure information services to national and defense intelligence components around the world. All U.S. Government TS-SCI networks run off of JWICS.

NGANet: NGA's TS-SCI network.

NMIS: NRO Management Information System (NMIS) is NRO's Top Secret network. NMIS is also referred to as GWAN (Government Wide Area Network).

NSANet: NSA's internal classified network.

SCION: Sensitive Compartmented Information Operational Network (SCION) is the FBI's TS-SCI network.

Stone Ghost: The Top Secret network run by DIA to facilitate information sharing and exchange with Commonwealth partners. It is used by Australia, Canada, the United Kingdom, and the United States. This capability may also be referred to a "Q-Lat" or "Quad link." Stone Ghost does not carry Intelink-TS.

PHONE AND FAX

Classified Faxes: Secure telephones (STUs and STEs) can transmit classified faxes, when connected to an approved fax machine.

DSN: Defense Switched Network (DSN) is the network that transmits secure and non-secure voice, data, and video teleconferencing information, including for STEs, STUs, and SIPRNet.

GETS: Government Emergency Telecommunications Service (GETS) is a national phone network that is designed to provide voice communications in an emergency or disaster. It uses standard long-distance, local, and federally-leased telephone networks.

NOIWON: National Operations and Intelligence Watch Officer Network (NOIWON) is a dedicated secure telephone system with a conferencing capability, for the rapid exchange and sharing of high interest and time-sensitive information between Washington, D.C.-area operations centers.

NSTS: NSA/CSS Secure Telephone System (NSTS) is a stand-alone secure telephone system that allows conversation up to the TS-SCI level. IC entities call these phones by different names, such as grey, white, or green phones, although these colors do not always reflect the actual color of the telephone unit.

STE: Secure Terminal Equipment (STEs) are telephones that can carry secure conversations. STEs are replacing STUs, although STUs are still in common use.

STU: Secure Telephone Units (STUs) are telephones that can carry secure conversations. STUs can also function as regular telephones when the Crypto Ignition Key (CIK) is not inserted.

WashFax: A secure fax system intended for use within the D.C. Beltway.

Comprehensive IC support to customers is a key ODNI focus. We accomplish that by developing and implementing policy and by helping customers reach into and work with the IC. Direct points of contact within ODNI for general assistance, information technology, public affairs, and security are provided below.

77

INTELLIGENCE
COMMUNITY ASSISTANCE

General Assistance

Please call the general assistance number listed above for any question about the Intelligence Community or accessing intelligence. As part of the ODNI's consumer focus, we have provided channel managers—single points of responsibility who help orchestrate, connect, and advocate on behalf of the IC's relationship with its partners and with intelligence consumers.

Chief Information Office

The Office of the Associate Director of National Intelligence and Chief Information Officer (ADNI & CIO) is responsible for issues relating to managing the IC's information technology by:

- Using technology to facilitate the free flow of intelligence, including developing current policies and investigating future technologies.
- Managing technology to support the business of intelligence and to reduce duplication and waste.
- Standardizing information technology and procedures on acquiring and applying intelligence-related information technology.
- Designing, building, and operating information technology tools that serve all intelligence users, instead of having each organization develop their own competing tools.

PUBLIC AFFAIRS OFFICE

The Office of the Director of National Intelligence Public Affairs Office (PAO) serves as the lead organization for the DNI for all internal and external strategic communications. The PAO develops communications strategies to help disseminate key messages to four principal target audiences—the internal workforce, members of the media, the general public, and other interested external stakeholders. The organization acts as the "front door" for individual, public, and media requests; maintains and operates content for the ODNI web sites on the Internet and Intranet systems; and, facilitates all public responses and appearances of the ODNI leadership. The PAO consists of a front office and three distinct areas of specialty: the Media Relations Division (MRD); the Public Outreach Division (POD); and, the Internal Communications Division (ICD). All three branches work in coordination to ensure that messages are consistent and are disseminated to the appropriate audience in a timely manner.

SPECIAL SECURITY CENTER

The ODNI's Special Security Center is responsible for developing clear, uniform, IC-wide security standards and practices to govern such issues as access to facilities, electronic access to systems and databases, and clearance of personnel.

ODNI security professionals can help consumers with:

- Training, by:
  - Providing or directing to courses in physical security, information systems security, and classification management.
  - Providing a Sensitive Compartmented Information (SCI) orientation seminar.
- Clearances, by:
  - Providing access to Scattered Castles, the IC repository of clearance and access approval information, to easily verify the clearances of employees in other organizations.
  - Providing entrance to Special Access Programs (SAPs), as needed, through the Controlled Access Program Coordination Office (CAPCO).
- Security, by:
  - Helping develop and implement security policies for handling and protecting intelligence information.
  - Providing guidance on how to build, accredit, and maintain Sensitive Compartmented Information Facilities (SCIFs).
  - Documenting and investigating unauthorized disclosures of intelligence information.

81

REFERENCE

GLOSSARY

All-Source: Intelligence product or analysis that uses all the sources of intelligence available to come to a conclusion, instead of just relying on one primary source. This may also be referred to as multi-INT reporting.

Compartmented Intelligence: National intelligence information under a control system and only available to designated individuals.

Cultural Intelligence: Knowledge resulting from all-source analysis of cultural factors, which assists in anticipating the actions of people or groups of people.

Expeditionary Intelligence: Intelligence in support of an armed force organized to accomplish a specific objective in a foreign country.

Information Assurance: Protecting information's confidentiality, integrity, and availability.

National Intelligence: According to the Intelligence Reform and Terrorism Prevention Act of 2004 (IRTPA), National Intelligence and the term 'intelligence related to national security' refer to all intelligence, regardless of the source from which derived and including information gathered within or outside the U.S., that:
- Pertains, as determined consistent with any guidance issued by the President, to more than one U.S. Government agency; and
- That involves:
  - Threats to the U.S., its people, property, or interests;
  - The development, proliferation, or use of weapons of mass destruction; or
  - Any other matter bearing on U.S. national homeland security.

Sensitive Compartmented Information (SCI): Classified information concerning or derived from intelligence sources, methods, or analytical processes requiring handling exclusively within formal access control systems established by the DNI.

Sensitive Compartmented Information Facility (SCIF): An accredited area where Sensitive Compartmented Information may be stored, used, discussed, and/or processed. Only those IC Agencies with SCIF Accreditation Authority may officially accredit facilities to handle, process, and store SCI materials.

Unauthorized Disclosure: A communication or physical transfer of classified information to an unauthorized recipient.

ABBREVIATIONS AND ACRONYMS

ADNI: Associate Director of National Intelligence

AF ISR: Air Force Intelligence, Surveillance and Reconnaissance Agency (formerly AIA)

AFMIC: Armed Forces Medical Intelligence Center (now NCMI)

AIN: Agency Internet (CIA)

AIA: Air Intelligence Agency (now Air Force ISR Agency)

ARC: Analytic Resource Catalog

AYP: Analyst Yellow Pages

CAPCO: Controlled Access Program Coordination Office

CapNet: Capitol Network

CBRN: Chemical, biological, radiological, and nuclear

CIK: Crypto Ignition Key

CD: Counterintelligence Division (FBI)

CIA: Central Intelligence Agency

CIO: Chief Information Officer

CNO: Chief of Naval Operations

COMINT: Communications Intelligence

CSS: Central Security Service (of the National Security Agency / Central Security Service)

CTD: Counterterrorism Division (FBI)

CWAN: Contractor Wide Area Network (NRO)

DCIA: Director of the Central Intelligence Agency

DDI: Director of Defense Intelligence

DDNI: Deputy Director of National Intelligence

DEA: Drug Enforcement Administration

DH: Directorate for Human Intelligence (DIA)

DHS: Department of Homeland Security

DI: Directorate of Intelligence (CIA, FBI)

DI: Directorate for Analysis (DIA)

DIA: Defense Intelligence Agency

DIAC: Defense Intelligence Analysis Center (DIA)

DIOCC: Defense Intelligence Operations Coordination Center (DIA)

DIRINT: Director of Intelligence (Marine Corps)

DNI: Director of National Intelligence

DNRO: Director of the National Reconnaissance Office

DoD: Department of Defense

DoDIIS: Department of Defense Intelligence Information System

DOE: Department of Energy

DS: Directorate of Support (CIA)

DS: Directorate for Information Management and Chief Information Officer (DIA)

DS&T: Directorate of Science and Technology (CIA)

DSN: Defense Switch Network

DT: Directorate for MASINT and Technical Collection (DIA)

DTRA: Defense Threat Reduction Agency

ELINT: Electronic Intelligence

FBI: Federal Bureau of Investigation

FIG: Field Intelligence Group (FBI)

FISINT: Foreign Instrumentation Signals Intelligence

FIST: Field Intelligence Support Team (Coast Guard)

GDIP: General Defense Intelligence Program

GEOINT: Geospatial Intelligence

GETS: Government Emergency Telecommunications Service

GMII: Global Maritime Intelligence Integration

GWAN: Government Wide Area Network (NRO; aka NMIS)

HOCNet: HUMINT Operational Communications Network (DoD)

HPSCI: House Permanent Select Committee on Intelligence

HSC: Homeland Security Council

HSDN: Homeland Security Data Network (DHS)

HSIN: Homeland Security Information Network (DHS)

HSPD: Homeland Security Presidential Directive

HUMINT: Human Intelligence

I&A: Office of Intelligence & Analysis (DHS)

IC: Intelligence Community

ICC: Intelligence Coordination Center (Coast Guard)

IMINT: Imagery Intelligence

IN: Office of Intelligence and Counterintelligence (DOE)

INFOSEC: Information Security

INR: Bureau of Intelligence and Research (State)

INRISS: INR Intelligence Support System (State)

INSCOM: Intelligence and Security Command (Army)

IOB: Intelligence Oversight Board

IRTPA: Intelligence Reform and Terrorism Prevention Act of 2004

ISC: Information Sharing Council

ISE: Information Sharing Environment

ISR: Intelligence, Surveillance, and Reconnaissance

ITFC: Iraq Threat Finance Cell

J2: Directorate for Intelligence, Joint Staff (DoD)

JDISS: Joint Deployable Intelligence Support System

JMIC: Joint Military Intelligence College (DIA – now NDIC)

JTTF: Joint Terrorism Task Force

JWICS: Joint Worldwide Intelligence Communications System

LEO: Law Enforcement Online
MASINT: Measurement and Signature Intelligence

MCIA: Marine Corps Intelligence Activity

MI: Military Intelligence

MIP: Military Intelligence Program

MSIC: Missile and Space Intelligence Center (MSIC)

NAIC: National Air Intelligence Center (Air Force – now NASIC)

NASIC: National Air and Space Intelligence Center (Air Force – formerly NAIC)

NCIX: National Counterintelligence Executive

NCMI: National Center for Medical Intelligence (formerly AFMIC)

NCPC: National Counterproliferation Center

NCS: National Clandestine Service

NCTC: National Counterterrorism Center

NDIC: National Defense Intelligence College (DIA – formerly JMIC)

NFIP: National Foreign Intelligence Program (now NIP)

NGA: National Geospatial-Intelligence Agency (formerly NIMA)

NGIC: National Ground Intelligence Center (Army)

NIC: National Intelligence Council (ODNI)

NIC-C: National Intelligence Coordination Center (ODNI)

NIE: National Intelligence Estimate

NIP: National Intelligence Program (formerly NFIP)

NIPRNet: Non-Secure Internet Protocol Router Network (DoD)

NIPF: National Intelligence Priorities Framework

NIMA: National Imagery and Mapping Agency (now NGA)

NJTTF: National Joint Terrorism Task Force

NMEC: National Media Exploitation Center

NMIC: National Maritime Intelligence Center (Navy/USCG)

NMIS: NRO Management Information System (aka GWAN)

NOIWON: National Operations and Intelligence Watch Officer Network

NOL: NCTC Online

NRO: National Reconnaissance Office

NSA: National Security Agency

NSA/CSS: National Security Agency / Central Security Service

NSB: National Security Branch (FBI)

NSC: National Security Council

NSOC: National Security Operations Center (NSA)

NSPD: National Security Presidential Directive

NSTS: NSA/CSS Secure Telephone System

NTOC: NSA/CSS Threat Operations Center

NVTC: National Virtual Translation Center

ODNI: Office of the Director of National Intelligence

OIA: Office of Intelligence and Analysis (Department of the Treasury)

OMB: Office of Management and Budget

ONCIX: Office of the National Counterintelligence Executive

ONI: Office of Naval Intelligence (Navy)

ONSI: Office of National Security Intelligence (DEA)

OPNAV N2: Director for Naval Intelligence (Navy)

OSC: Open Source Center

OSINT: Open Source Intelligence

PDDNI: Principal Deputy Director of National Intelligence

PFIAB: President's Foreign Intelligence Advisory Board (now PIAB)

PIAB: President's Intelligence Advisory Board and Intelligence Oversight Board (formerly PFIAB)

PM-ISE: Program Manager for the Information Sharing Environment

SAP: Special Access Program

SCI: Sensitive Compartmented Information

SCIF: Sensitive Compartmented Information Facility

SCION: Sensitive Compartmented Information Operational Network (FBI)

SIGINT: Signals Intelligence

SIPRNet: Secure Internet Protocol Router Network

SSCI: Senate Select Committee on Intelligence

STE: Secure Terminal Equipment

STU: Secure Telephone Unit

TIDE: Terrorist Identities Datamart Environment (NCTC)

TS-SCI: Top Secret-Sensitive Compartmented Information

TSC: Terrorist Screening Center

TSDB: Terrorist Screening Database

UFAC: Underground Facilities Analysis Center

UGF: Underground Facility

USCG: U.S. Coast Guard

USCG-ICC: U.S. Coast Guard Intelligence Coordination Center

USMC: United States Marine Corps

WMD: Weapon of Mass Destruction

WMDD: Weapons of Mass Destruction Directorate (FBI)

95

INDEX